A Roomier Place to Call Home

A journal of prayers

Written and painted by Caryn Evans

Edited by Gene McKelvey

Cover art: "Separation"

Caring Publications, LLC

Copyright © 2014 by Caryn Evans

All rights reserved. This book or any portion thereof may not be reproduced or used in any manner whatsoever without the express written permission of the publisher except for the use of brief quotations in a book review or scholarly journal.

First Printing: 2014

ISBN: 978-0-578-14559-4

Caring Publications, LLC
P.O. Box 120
2815 100th St., Urbandale, IA 50322

Contents

Acknowledgements	1
Foreword	2
Preface	3
Introduction	4
Plans and Hearts	6
Exhale	15
In Between	38
Passage of Mother	49

Acknowledgements

I thank God who talks with me every day and listens to my questions.

I dedicate this book to my husband, Bill Evans, my constant love and source of encouragement.

I thank Suzanne Stout and Debra Garner for their spiritual guidance over the past year. Suzanne encouraged me to listen to my heart and Debra taught me that one could pray with a paintbrush and a box of watercolors. Both taught me that creativity is one of God's gifts to humanity.

Thanks to Gene McKelvey for his editing and design skills, and for introducing me to the visual arts many years ago. His love for God is a blessing to all who work with him; and his patience and knowledge on how to put this book together has been a gift. I thank his family for the time shared on this project.

Foreword

Like most people, I live from day to day expecting a repeat of the day before. During the last year, life shook me awake. The loss of loved ones, injury and illness within my family, and retirement after 52 years of work led me on a journey into creativity. GOD knew I would be challenged by not going to work every day. HE inspired me to sit in front of the computer and talk with him. HE sent a friend to give me a paint brush, and I immediately felt obliged to talk with HIM in color. If this sounds strange to you, it is even stranger for me, but it works.

"Roads"

Through watercolors, GOD reintroduced me to the love of beauty I experienced as a child, and it reflects in my watercolor paintings. GOD encourages me to listen with my heart to the stories of old and new friends. Together, we examine the ordinary and the extraordinary. We reflect on newly made friendships and on the renewal of old friendships. GOD also teaches me to listen with my heart to my own stories. These stories become my written and painted prayers.

This is my story of going to work for GOD, sharing newly found gifts and finally feeling like I landed the "right" job

Caryn Evans
August, 2014

Preface

Left: "Dreaming 3"
Right: "Tree in the wilderness"

    I once heard of an exercise practiced by women in 18th century England. They drew a balance sheet in the morning, creating a column on the left side listing expected events for the day and a column on the right with the details of how the events of the day actually unfolded. Over the last year, I learned the value of this exercise. No matter what I expect to happen during any given day, what actually happens is out of my control. I find that unexpected joys, tragedies, and bumps in the road test my faith and my facility at repeatedly turning my life over to GOD. I recognize how deeply my life is transformed when I welcome CHRIST into my life. This book uses prayer to journal my story of renewing relationships with GOD and CHRIST while living in the moment.

Introduction

"Notes and knots"

    In retirement, I am ridding my house of belongings that no longer are of use to me. What I still need I keep. Those items whose time of service for me has ended go to those who need them. Whatever is determined as junk goes into the garbage. This is a time of transition for me and the cleaning I am doing includes ridding my heart of old perceived injuries. As I grow older, I understand the need to provide GOD a roomier place to call home. That place is my heart.

    Throwing things out is hard work and I rely on GOD'S help to sort. While we sort, I pray and post my reflections on social media. My prayers are created in the moment. I pray for us all as we learn the truth of living in the world. In praying, I become a different person—one who delights in GOD'S love and presence. Praying leads me to see CHRIST in all I meet and I am blessed.

I accepted an invitation to a class on praying in color. I was given paper, a paint brush and a box of watercolors. The minute I laid the brush on the paper, something inside my soul came alive and creativity seized me. Some say that grief used wisely turns into creativity. GOD is full of surprises. My grief, that once produced only sadness, now charges me with creative abilities previously unknown. My soul is now a sacred space, a space where GOD and I engage in a dance of light.

I believe sacredness calls us to be sensual. Visual art, music, crafts, dance, writing, etc. are gifts GOD gives us to delight others and remind us of who created us. I find sacredness in the most unexpected places. When I paint, my hand, guided by mystery, surprises me.

Occasionally, color refuses to adhere to areas on the paper. The resulting white spaces signal me to breathe out the chaos of the moment. Objects or ideas emerging from the paintings encourage me to stop and look. Learning how to look at and read a painting exhilarates me.

The messiness of watercolor and the messiness of life seem to run parallel. When I approach the paper, watercolor gives me permission to express my emotions. I experiment with the paints and say "What if?" The discovery for me is that I carry this creative approach into my life with others. When I make a mistake and the paint goes everywhere, I see how my words, spoken or written in haste, lead to unintended drama. In moments of thoughtfulness, placement of paint on the paper slows me down and I consider in prayer various options for being in the world as GOD intended. I am a beginner in the practice of painting. I am a beginner in finding sacredness in all things. Journaling through prayer, in words and paint, opens my heart. GOD is assured of a roomier place to call home.

Caryn Evans

Plans and Hearts

All stories begin somewhere. This one starts on a summer Sunday in August of 2013. The day burst at the seams with plans—first church, then a picnic at the family farm, followed by a bonfire in the evening to smoke away the bugs. Those were the items on the joy list that day. But the joy was erased with the ring of the phone and a voice on the other end saying, "We believe you better come. It's taken all night to find you, but your brother-in-law drove into a building during a blinding rainstorm, and we think you better come." My brother-in-law was critically injured and was in a Springfield, Missouri trauma hospital. The prognosis for recovery was not positive. We were there for eight days with no sign of his improvement. It was during this time my journey in prayer began in earnest.

"Protecting the heart"

JOURNAL ENTRIES FROM THE TRIP TO SPRINGFIELD

08/04/13 — After eight hours, we arrived safely. Joel is thrilled to see his mom. Injuries include broken hips, a broken leg, a broken wrist, but no apparent head trauma. We will know more tomorrow about neck and spine. With luck, we found a hotel close to hospital. The hospital is huge and statues of saints are everywhere. This is a good sign.

08/05/13 — My request for prayers from you has been fulfilled. I am learning to say the Rosary to keep anxiety at bay. We will certainly know more about his condition today

08/06/13 — Again, we need prayers. Surgery is not likely until tomorrow, as Joel needs another day to stabilize. His coworkers visited yesterday and provided needed comfort for us all. They are taking care of his cats, his garden, and watching his home. He is blessed by the kindness they have shown.

08/06/13 — Joel is slow to stabilize. The hospital is fantastic and is doing everything they can. We visited the site of the accident today and Bill spoke with the police. No one can say exactly how the accident happened.

08/06/13 — The Ozarks are beautiful. We are hanging around the hotel tonight hoping we do not get a call. Your prayers are so welcome. We cannot thank GOD enough for his gifts even those we cannot understand.

08/07/13 — We continue to experience synchronicity on this journey. Nearly everyone we talk with seems to know Joel or have some useful information for us. We ate lunch at Joel's place of employment and visited with his coworkers. They provide help and support to us. The doctors placed Joel on a ventilator today to make breathing easier. Thanks for the prayers from back home. Today, I determined that I will talk with GOD myself.

"Praying for healing"

08/07/13 — **Almighty and everlasting God**, You are the source of love that never ends. Thank You for those who bring us back to You when we are tired, sick, and feel lost. Your disciples are at work and we pray for Your blessing on them. Grant us all a healing night that we may waken refreshed and ready to do Your work as Christ taught us. In Your Son's name we pray, amen.

08/07/13 — **God**, when we were children we would often lie on the grass and gaze at the clouds, trying to put names to the shapes. With our faces bathed with light from the sun, and our bodies touched by wind, wild clover, and dandelions, we felt the world was perfect. The light, the fragrances, and the warmth were the evidence of God's presence. We gifted ourselves moments to reflect and imagine. Sometimes our innocent thanksgiving took the form of squeals of delight and laughter. Today, we need time to give ourselves over to that childish delight. Memories are often like clouds. They morph, move, and give us joy and moments of solitude as we ponder their meaning. May we treasure every single memory. Amen

"Dreaming 2"

08/07/13 — Every bit of news we have gotten today shows Joel progressing. He is stabilizing. He cannot yet be released for surgery as he is still under sedation. This hospital is faith in action and you are prayer warriors. Such a blessing to each of us.

08/09/13 — The social worker who met with us today looked and sounded exactly like Mr. Rogers. I finally asked if others had seen the resemblance. He said he leaves his sweater at home. I grinned all through the interview.

8/11/13 — Joel is still not off the ventilator. We hated to leave, but must return home. His lungs are distressed and he still needs surgery. Please continue your prayers for healing.

08/11/13 — Thanks to everyone for prayers. This week we reflected and lived in the moment. I had a chance to enjoy strangers' private gardens and intentional public gardens. GOD was with us every moment and we are changed by our experience at Mercy Hospital in Springfield. I saw radical welcome practiced by everyone.

08/13/13 — **Holy One**, the day is drawing to a close. It greeted us with mysteries and memories. We thank YOU, GOD for both. I love the moments of surrender when nothing matters but awareness of YOU. Thank YOU for YOUR presence. We pray in CHRIST'S name, amen.

08/14/13 — **O LORD**, My thoughts turn to our big old house on Harrison Avenue. Kathy and I read by flashlight after the sun went down and we cooled beside a big green window fan.

Mom stacked records on our hi-fi and we listened to great music as we fell asleep. The music was great, but, it was the night bugs—locusts, grasshoppers, and bees in the neighbor's peach trees that made the greatest music of all.

It is fun to know that although my siblings have memories of growing up that are individual, we collectively share the sounds of summer. Thank you, LORD, for the sounds of a summer's eve. Amen.

08/14/13 — **Bless us God** as we rest from a day's labor. Bless all who may be struggling with health or other of life's challenges. We pray for another day to do Your work, always remembering that love is an active verb. In Your Son's name, we pray, amen.

08/15/13 — **Dear Lord**, morning sounds, and smells are as sweet as the sounds of evening. We live in a world surrounded with art created by the greatest artist of all. Thank You for a day of beauty. Amen.

08/15/13 — **O Lord**, we give You thanks for one more day with loved ones, and for health and healing. These gifts transform us. Thank You for moments of silliness and devotion. You are the heart of our hearts. We feel Your presence waking or sleeping. Give us clear vision to stay in the moment and do Your will. In Christ's name, we pray, amen

8/16/13 — **God**, You were with me today when I made mistakes and yet You love me still. You created moments of beauty and joy, and though undeserving, You offered Yourself to me unconditionally. Give me courage to be grace filled and constant in my love for You. As darkness draws near, I am certain of Your steady presence through the night. Bless those I love and those I have not yet come to love. Let my heart be open enough to welcome You in all Your manifestations. In Christ's name, I pray, amen

08/17/13 — **Gracious God**, thanks for the joy and gifts shared with us today. We laughed and danced with abandon as we celebrated Your saints. We know that just as You are with us in joy, You are with us in sorrow. Give us the strength required to face difficult times. May we continue to serve You. May we forgive ourselves when we fall short of YOUR desires for us. Watch over us as we rest and depend on meeting YOU in the morning. Amen.

08/18/13 — **GOD of all creation**, breathe forgiveness into my life. Old hurts sometimes open as new wounds and the pain is heavy. I always question why and I pray for understanding that sometimes the only answer is "because." Amen.

08/18/13 — **GOD**, my life has been rich with blessings and I will recite them as one says the alphabet. YOU are a master weaver and I live for the time when the whole pattern is revealed. In the meantime, grant to me grace and the goodness to pass it along. In the name of CHRIST, amen.

08/19/13 — **Author of all**, we ask that YOU read the words etched on hearts. Words we didn't know were there. May the words that we speak do no harm. May we be CHRIST to all we meet. We give thanks for spaces in our day when we hear the still, small, voice affirming we are worthy of love. Amen.

08/19/13 — **Gracious GOD**, YOU made this day for living life to its fullest. Thank YOU for the joy of found friends and for keeping them safe over the years. We pray for those who are suffering and feel hopeless. Grant them good friends to help them see that CHRIST is alive and sharing their burdens. Give us a peaceful rest and may we wake again to do the work YOU have put before us. Amen.

08/21/13 — **Gracious GOD**, I would have prayed sooner today but the sunrise and songs of the birds distracted me; and then I paused in traffic while an EMT crew safely delivered a baby. When I got to work, all the good parking places were gone and so I walked through soft, new, moist grass to reach the door. My computer crashed and downtime allowed me to pass some time outside, and then I remembered to pray. This day, I noticed verbs, adjectives, adverbs and the nouns in action. The day astounded me. Amen.

08/22/13 — **Eternal ruler**, You keep us on our toes. Adaptive behavior seems to be the lesson of the month. Thank You for Bill's safe arrival in Springfield and for his giving heart.

I know how much he suffers, and how he seeks strength from You. He makes rough places in Joel's healing process straight. With You, he is not alone. It is quiet in the house but You watch over me. May I wake in the morning confident in Your mercy and grace. In Your Son's name, I pray, amen.

08/22/13 — **Blessed Creator**, thank You for joy in the morning. There is time for coffee on the deck and gazing at the trees. Your birds may pay me a visit if I stay quiet. Teach me to slow down so that Your creations become a sketch on my heart available for viewing when the winds of winter keep me away. Amen.

08/24/13 — **Gracious God**, I give You thanks for another day. I have plans for my time today, but I am learning that we may not have the same plan. Instead of filling every moment with activity, I will set aside time to linger with You and Your words so that I may receive direction on how to be a disciple of Christ in this day and age. My desire is to love and to be loved as Christ shared in the Great Commandment. Amen.

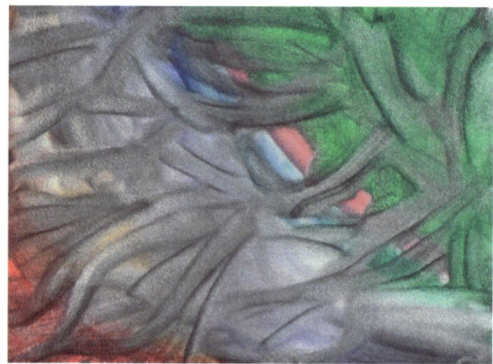

"Roots 1"

08/24/13 — **GOD**, I give up wishing I were the one who fit in or who was chosen first. I understand that YOU made me unique, just as YOU made all of YOUR children. YOU may have done so to amuse YOURSELF, but the result is a vibrant, interesting world in which creation continuously occurs. I am especially happy tonight for having shared the morning with people who encourage me to claim, "I am beautiful and wonderfully made". May our gifts rise to the surface and glue themselves into our consciousness. May we never be the last to learn that we made a difference. In CHRIST'S name, I pray. Amen.

08/26/15 — **Dear GOD**, YOU are my best friend. My prayers are but a summary of the long discussions we hold during the day. We are admonished to "Pray without ceasing." Since I started paying attention, my thoughts are focused on YOUR will and not mine.

I now notice what I normally miss. I see YOU at work in all I meet. I see that within my community new life is happening for others and me. So, thank YOU for YOUR feedback to relax and give prayer a chance. Amen.

08/28/13 — **GOD**, today was a blessing. Sharing with friends who took different routes to find YOU is exciting. Even more exciting is learning that there is more to us than how we are labeled. The gift of story is enriching my relationship with YOU. Let my heart always have room for more pages upon which to write the sacred of others. Amen

08/30/13 MIRACLES HAPPEN

Bill got the guardianship of Joel through the court, got banking done and now Joel can be moved to the hospital that he needs to be in. Thank you for your prayers. I think Joel will be pleased.

FINAL OBSERVATION ON JOEL

Joel recovered from his accident and is living in his home. Praise to God.

Exhale

09/01/13 — **Bread of Heaven**, we have come to YOU with the best of intentions and we are welcomed and loved. We are perfectly made and yet we sometimes forget to be who we are. Help us remember that intention without action saddens YOU. Today we will act in the ways YOU have shown us and we will eat again the bread of heaven. People will come to us not knowing the invitation YOU offer for eternal life. Let us respond by sharing YOUR body and the cup of remembrance.

We give YOU thanks for the gifts of ministry we have received. We begin again to breathe in YOUR SPIRIT and share the table. Amen.

09/01/13 — **GOD of all**, night has drawn shades on the day and we await the breath of sleep. We have done nothing today to earn YOUR grace and yet YOU pardon us. When the air of morning caresses us awake, may we become one with YOU and open ourselves to make a home for those who hunger and thirst for a place at someone's table. We offer a meal that is eternal and one where the table is set for more. We pray that Mary, the mother of JESUS, will carry our petitions to YOU and that she will wrap us in her mantle of humility and hospitality and deliver us. We seek a new day where we may continue our journey to achieve the habit of radical hospitality. Amen.

09/02/13 — **LORD of the dance**, we have so many reasons to dance today. Our dancing shoes are fresh and ready to take us to new places. They are gifts from YOU. We hear YOU call our names and in joy, we turn in delight. We beg YOU for lessons on how to be a new creation and YOU respond that we are made as intended. We are relieved that we already know our dance steps and they please YOU. YOU ask us to whirl into the world and gather the lonely, lame, unacknowledged others and bring them to YOUR feast. YOU will seat them at YOUR table, give them drink from YOUR cup, bread from body and share the beat of YOUR heart. In time, they too will dance as intended and go out in delight to fulfill YOUR will. We thank YOU for the gift of dance and the reassurance that all steps are perfect. In YOUR name, we pray, amen.

"Dancing"

09/03/13 — **Patient One**, we welcome a new day when we may try again to leave our childhood fears behind and move forward in trust. The glue of the past is sticky and difficult to remove. The strings of glue show up even after we have washed and washed our hands. When I am stuck, I fail to act in love, kindness, and grace. My prayer today is that I remember that YOU are the GOD of all ages and when we hurt as a child, YOU cried with us, and as an adult, YOU understand where we have been. I am blessed with those YOU provide who comfort and love me, glue, and all. May I have a glue-free day and place my trust in YOU. In the name of CHRIST, my SAVIOR, amen.

09/03/13 — **GOD of peace**, some days, like today, we find YOUR voice in music. We marvel at Samuel Barber's *Adagio for Strings*, holding our breath for fear we will miss a note. We weep at hearing Eva Cassidy sing *Fields of Gold*. Samuel and Eva two of YOUR many saints, inspire us to stop, and really listen. YOU drop in to speak to us in a language that eliminates the need for spoken word. Lovely St. Cecelia guards the language of music, making sure that even those who cannot hear can feel the beat. We remind ourselves today that losing ourselves in the common experience of music leaves room for the possibility that music is the vehicle for peace. In the name of CHRIST, I sing YOUR praise. Amen.

09/04/13 — **LORD of thought**, I am often bewildered by my feelings. Just when I feel my world is perfect, a thought creeps into my head and the thought is framed as a question. "What more can I do to serve YOU?" Then I hear YOUR voice. It is always the same answer, "Fear not, for I am with you and the risks you take I take too." How long will it take me to believe that YOU are always there? As an adolescent, I yearned to know YOU more. I still have that longing, but fear it is too late to acquire deeper knowledge of YOU. There is that word again, "fear." Does fear ever leave us or is it required to give our lives to YOU? Alternatively, have I ministered in my own way, and am I too blind to see? In CHRIST'S name, I pray, amen.

09/04/13 — **GOD of sacred spaces**, I observe that space becomes sacred when acts of mercy, grace, and joy mark themselves like fingerprints on copper. Moments become sacred when we pledge our hearts and faithfulness to another. When we share our deepest thoughts through prayer, or bring a stranger to YOUR SON'S table and offer the hospitality given to us so long ago, sacredness becomes real. In CHRIST'S name, amen.

09/05/13 OBSERVATION

The afternoon is lazy; the wind too tired to dance.

Frogs sing softly, barely able to harmonize with locusts.

The grass hardened into shards, no longer tickles my feet.

Summer is sleepy and ready for a nap.

09/06/13 **LORD of magnificence**, praise to artisans whose hands coaxed beauty out of stone. Praise for glass so fragile, it might have been blown and colored by angels. Praise for the arches that draw our eyes upward to see depictions of YOUR moments of joy and YOUR hours of suffering for our sakes. Praise for ones who honored YOU in carvings that seem to come alive when we kneel before them. But LORD, we thank YOU for YOUR presence, no matter how or where we find YOU. Amen.

09/07/13 — **JESUS**, YOUR miracles refresh me like rain in the desert. Spending time with YOU in prayer this morning, with a saint who knows the struggle I have had turning to YOU, was a gift that could only have been sent by YOU. Seeking YOU is a journey that sometimes requires a guide and YOU sent a good one. Thanks be to YOU, CHRIST, for helping find my way home. Amen.

"Joy"

09/07/13 — **Dear God**, A question: What is Your favorite part of the day? Opening Your paint box and choosing reds, and pinks and gold in the morning; or the yellows and oranges tinged with red at night. It is too much to imagine that You chose the colors at random. The idea that sunrises and sunsets bursting with color happen in every part of the world comforts me. Sometimes, we chose to scribble on Your canvas and create horrendous hues. Yet, for a few moments every day, everywhere, Your paintbrush gives us the ability to imagine a different world—one that is colored in peace. Amen.

09/07/13 — **Heavenly one**, I spoke today with one who walks in the steps of Your son. She has nothing of material value and so she uses her time and talents to ensure that a neighbor will have his home and pets to return to when he is able. I asked her why she would make sure everything was kept clean and safe and she replied "It's what you do for a neighbor." Her stewardship is faithful. Let me be as faithful as she. Amen.

09/08/13 — **God of salvation**, when we come to dine at Your table today, the meal is an extravagant offering. The bread and the cup are the ultimate sacrifice to feed all who hunger and thirst. Your table extends as more come to believe in Christ and come with grace in their hearts. May we need to add chairs to the table today. Amen.

09/08/13 — **God of imagination and journey**, the saints of First Christian Church were surely weeping with joy today as the congregation affirmed and pledged to be Christ to each other and the world. 125 years of leading the community in peace and justice issues moved us to take a formal step. You were there with us as we discerned what Jesus would expect us to do if we truly follow his example. The feeling of complete embrace took place as we participated in the act of affixing our names to the statement of who we are. We are YOUR people and this is how we choose to be in ministry.

In the name of YOUR son, JESUS, who fed the hungry, healed the lame, and dared to associate with the unacceptable others, we declare that we are an open community of worship, nurture, and service. Amen and amen!

AFFIRMATION: "This prayer expresses the heart of First Christian Church Des Moines, and I thank Caryn Evans for giving us prayerful words to reflect on yesterday's action!" ~*Ryan Arnold, Senior Pastor at First Christian Church (Disciples of Christ)*

09/09/13 — **Spirit of life's journeys**, sometimes we are frightened and sad. Things don't work as we planned. An ache in our hearts takes hold and in the midst of the pain, we find opportunity. Because of an ache, I have two children who fill me with a type of love I could never have imagined. Because of an ache, I focused on education and the places it took me. Because of an ache, I met the love of my life. Because of an ache, I have fascinating grandchildren. Because of an ache, I have learned to find my way to YOU. Because of an ache, I am who I am today. I thank YOU today for things that cause us to have places in our hearts that once felt like stone but now are threads in beautiful tapestries woven from what happened because of an ache. Amen.

09/10/13 — **GOD of lost gifts**, I came into the world singing and I hear music where there is none. One day I lost my voice and part of me retreated. Truth, the instrument no longer works. Yet I know that YOU still hear the songs coming from my heart and YOU recognize that the notes that are gone have been given to YOU. My hope is that the sounds of the lost notes are exquisite and are given as a gift to an angel who needed to sing in YOUR choir. Amen.

09/10/13 — **GOD of angel hair**, praying is often like a spider web. We start with one thought and we suddenly find ourselves wrapped in intricate thoughts that are completely unexpected. The light shining through a spider web reminds us of angel hair that we placed on our Christmas tree when we were children. I think about being that child who watched the spider weave the web and I smile to myself. My friends were afraid of spiders. They failed to see the beauty of the sticky web that trapped the flies that made summer picnics miserable. Mom always told us to leave the spiders alone as they had some purpose. I think of that when I open my spider-web frosted boxes of Christmas ornaments and find a handful of flies that didn't make it to our picnics. All things have a purpose, and only when we stand back and watch what is offered do we really have a sense of YOUR creativity. Amen.

"Adoration"

09/11/13 — **GOD**, YOU were with me when I gave my mother's caregiver directions to the nail salon. You heard me tell her which streets to take and which direction to turn at certain landmarks. What I hope YOU were not listening to was my confusion over right and left. I drive by memory and when I have to explain how I get somewhere, I really have to think hard to make it easy. I observed today that many times we move from memory—and lose our loved ones in the process. May I be very clear the next time I give directions to anyone? Thank YOU for loving us and helping us know right from left. However, I recognize that sometimes life takes us for a great ride as the result of poorly given human directions. Amen.

09/11/13 — **God**, Thank You for a lovely day. For friends and families bound together as tightly as ivy clings to a house. I pray again tonight for friends who are healing from surgery, broken bones and hearts. Lift the heaviness from hearts of parents who must accept a new normal for a child. Give them an extra embrace when they are overwhelmed. Bless those who have known a lifetime of harsh circumstances. May we do our best to be the protector of children who feel abandoned. Give us the necessary wisdom to make decisions that will lift those children out of despair and into safety. It is a lot to ask for, but friends are hurting and the truth is, praying is all I can do tonight. May something I have done today have the butterfly effect. While I wait, I thank You for Your mercy and grace. Amen.

09/12/13 — **Dearest God**, I knew when I stepped into Your garden that today was exceptional. The wind blew through trees and grass as if trying to blow summer away and make room for fall. I am in a new season of my life and You have given me a list of chores to perform. They don't all make sense to me, but I put my trust in You and will continue to enjoy the surprises You have in store. I pray tonight for family members and friends who are healing from surgery and injury.

I pray for families who are tired and weary from seeking a way back to wholeness. I pray for families that struggle to keep things the way they were rather than accept the way things are. I give thanks to You for children who need our continuing care. I pray especially for those whose world goes uncontrollably dark as if a fuse blew out. Too often, I have been in the dark place where I could not feel Your presence. It took people who were patient, kind, and willing to assume Your role to help turn the lights back up. Whatever role You ask of me tonight, tomorrow, or in the future, I willingly accept it. I accept my job tonight; to pray for those who haven't the energy. Amen.

09/12/13 A PRAYER FOR SKIMMERS

God: Love, Forgiveness, Mercy and Grace, are gifts from You to pass along. Amen.

09/14/13 — **God who tends the gardens of creativity**, thank You for sacred spaces given to us by people with prophetic imagination, patience and a belief that seeds and bulbs resurrect. Those beliefs are not shared through words on social media or on paper. They are planted in the dirt of Your Kingdom by gardeners, who take the risks inherent in creating a world where change flourishes. I know that taking risks in Your garden is a divine blessing. Amen.

09/14/13 OBSERVATION

To view a hummingbird hovering amazes us and we do all we can to attract them. We follow all the advice on what type of feeders are best and what liquid attracts them and yet, they stay away—except at that exact moment when we need to see a small miracle.

09/15/13 — **God**, I imagine if we were born sightless, our definition of beauty would be radically different. We might spend more time thanking You for the acts of beauty bestowed on us by others. I cursed You for years for the many flaws I found in the way I looked. The truth of beauty in me is my gift of intellectual curiosity, acceptance and encouragement to become who You imagined me to be. When we don't look at the internal beauty of another, we are sightless and more limited than we imagine the sightless to be.

"Open"

I can't change the world's view of beauty, but I can change myself to more closely be YOUR representative in a world obsessed with not being beautiful enough to be on the arm of one who expects physical beauty to last forever. Amen.

09/15/13 — **GOD**, rain came today and cool breezes returned to dance. The air is filled with sounds of workers hurrying to finish projects before the early frost, predicted by the locusts, arrives. The aroma from pots of soup and freshly baked bread will soon replace the smell of blooming flowers. But there is no season that causes us to replace YOU. YOU are permanently inscribed on our lives like the inscription on the inner band of a wedding ring. Speak to us in the language of falling leaves, early snowflakes, and smoke from campfires. We weather the changes in seasons and we ask that YOU help us weather the changes in life's circumstances, whatever they may be. From one who is moving into a new season of life let me renew my vow to be YOURS forever. Amen.

"Three leaves"

09/15/13 — **GOD**, I am praying tonight and thinking over my day. I spent the afternoon reading my prayers to my mother-in-law. She in turn shared prayers she has written over the years. We puzzled over the seeming oddness of people two generations apart asking the same life questions. Faith is not owned by any specific generation. It is available for all and we celebrated our personal quests to be a witness to the love of YOUR son. May YOU add YOUR blessing to the sharing of our words. Amen.

09/16/13 — **GOD who extends grace and mercy**, we pray for those who unexpectedly joined YOUR saints today. We pray for those who, out of their darkness destroyed lives, and for those who will need us to blanket them in love to stop the shivering from shock. Hearts are broken tonight all over the world. Piecing them back together may take a type of glue that is known only to YOU. My guess is that mixing the epoxy of love with the additive of reconciliation is the only way we will ever overcome the acceptance of violence as normal. We beg for comfort where there appears to be hopelessness. All saints on earth and in heaven working together are needed to make us whole. Grant us strength. Amen.

09/16/13 — **GOD**, tears flood my heart and eyes when I see and feel YOUR presence in strangers who seek me out at moments that make no sense. May I open my heart to them, listen to them and urge them to "Say more." May I be wise enough to ask "What do you think?" and honest enough to say, "I don't know." Use me as YOU will, but remember I am new here myself. Amen.

09/16/13 — **GOD**, this prayer is random, so bear with me. I like making an income and I like being creative in the workplace. Thanks for the gift of both. Also, I am thinking of getting some body art. To work in corporate America, it seems to be a requirement. I think I will find a place on my body that won't get all scrunched as I age and have it put there. Please let me know where that place would be. Amen.

09/17/13 — **Spirit of discovery**, every morning I lose my glasses. I race frantically through the house retracing my steps. My frantic efforts result from trying to do too many things before I leave for work. I get frustrated and I am reminded that if I put them in the same place every time I take them off, I could save time. That's too easy. In the moment of loss, I find the daily frantic search a reminder that YOU are never lost to me. Truth: YOU are in the same place I left YOU—always in my heart. Thanks for the consistent reminder of YOUR abiding presence. Amen.

09/17/13 — **CHRIST**, thank YOU for teaching us to pray. Our prayers go out for help, forgiveness, health, and the courage to engage in reconciliation. I confess that today was a day when I spoke first and prayed later. I try so hard to turn it the other way round, but when I am passionate about something, I forget that being still may be the best way to stay in community and the best way to pray. I will try for quietness tomorrow and hope for getting things done in the right order. Amen.

09/18/13 — **GOD**, tonight I ask that YOU bring YOUR peace and loving presence to my daughter and her friends as they prepare to say goodbye to a friend who in the span of six weeks has gone from being the mom of a nine-year old, and a treasured wife, to making plans for dying a good death. My heart aches at the loss of the vitality and goodness she has brought to all who know her. We know that CHRIST will welcome her with open arms, but how do I comfort my daughter in her grief? There are no words—only prayers. Amen.

09/19/13 — **GOD of dancing trees and final boughs**, today lightning struck my tree that danced for me the whole summer. When I saw the burn marks on the large branch and the same one on the trunk, I felt as if YOU were reminding me that even trees take a last bow at summer's end. The waltzing has stopped but the wind continues to blow across my face as if YOU are saying, "Just wait until YOU see what I have planned next." I thank YOU for swirling limbs and leaves that dance and rainbows that light up and adorn creation's ballroom. Amen.

09/22/13 OBSERVATION

The stark light of summer fades and pastels of fall creep in, soon to become more vivid and then gone with the wind and replaced by hoar frost announcing the silver of true cold found in snow.

09/22/13 — **LORD GOD**, may we parent like YOU. May the Light of CHRIST guide us through our lives on earth. May we love YOUR children when they are fresh and smooth and love them even more when they are shriveled with age. May we love them when we find that what we expected from parenthood was not what we got. May we love them when they retreat to places of darkness and we lose hope of reaching them. May we love them when they bring color into our lives, walking with abandon with shaved heads or sporting purple hair and body art.

"Under the sea"

We imagine that we are YOUR canvases and YOU create diversity among us to make the world interesting and exciting. We are people called to sing, dance, paint, crawl, and make noise as outward expressions of YOUR love. Regardless of how we move through the maze of life, we are assured that we will find YOU at the end ready and welcoming us into the communion of saints. We will recognize those saints as the parents, guided by CHRIST'S light, who raised us by choice—and by chance—and we will recognize YOU as the one who gave HIS SON so that the end of the maze we are released from captivity into newness of life. Amen.

09/22/13 — **Lord God**, we who write prayers are not saints. We are people trying to work our way through the rough waters of life by seeing what is true and what is good. We still drink beer and drink wine. We dance when the moment moves us and we sing even when the songs are unfamiliar. Wiser ones than we show us that Christ lived life in all the roughest places in all the roughest towns. And, we expect that he prayed often. Thank You for sending us the light of Christ so that we might see more clearly as we write. Amen.

09/24/13 — **God**, today I am not at my best and I am trying to pray and breathe through it. Only You know why I go to nights that are so dark. Every time it happens, I find You and am thankful to be lifted up to the light. I hate being out of control and yet, I know that by giving myself over to You I will find that the light is there. Thank You for loving me, and all Your children who have soul work to do. Amen.

09/25/13 — **Dear God**, we pray tonight for those who face recovery from injury or illness. We pray that Your loving wisdom and steady hands will guide those whose gift it is to heal. For those families who are anxious about outcomes we ask a special blessing. May they be released from the grips of a racing heart and the fear of the unknown. Your heart is the steady beat that makes us whole and Your embrace is the promise that when we breathe You are the breath of our lives—clean and pure and just waiting for us to inhale. Release us from fear and help us remember to take a breath. Amen.

09/26/13 — **Spirit of loveliness**, I give thanks tonight to You for making each of us perfect in Your sight. You know we are tangled up in what we think others expect. I once knitted a baby blanket, and when I took it to be blocked, the dry cleaner asked what it was supposed to be. For me it was an imperfect-perfect blanket to keep my baby warm. It did its job and she dragged it around until the yarn frayed. We are like that blanket, imperfect to some who see us, but perfect to YOU. YOU love us just as YOU made us. Let us never let our love for YOU fray at the edges and may we never let someone else impose their idea of perfection on us. Amen.

09/28/13— **Dear GOD**, I thank YOU for the gift of watercolors. Never did I imagine the poetry and prayers dwelling within. I Thank YOU for the gift givers who encourage new ways of seeing. I thank YOU for friends who share with me what they see when I put the colors on the paper. Creativity lives inside each of us and it is a gift from YOU that comes in all forms. Thank YOU for bringing friends to me who just happened to have a box of watercolors and a brush. Amen.

"Winter night sky"

09/30/13 — **Heavenly parent**, every day YOU give us reason for celebration. Yesterday was lovely in every way. YOU made weather perfect for dining outdoors. YOU took an ordinary sunset and made it extraordinary. Dusk came down like the scrim curtain on a stage, and stars gathered together to light the sky. It was a perfect day for celebrating relationships and relief from burdens. And today, what a day! It lies before us full of potential for celebrations and new discoveries. May my focus go where it needs to be, and may I, at the end of the day, thank YOU, GOD, for the celebrations big and small that came my way and that I didn't miss. Amen.

10/01/13 — **GOD of the morning**, the house is still, the hour early. I am blessed again to wake fully to YOUR presence. The possibilities and passion for acts of love and justice are endless. May I choose wisely and use my gifts to make a difference and answer cries for help. O GOD of all time let me be wise in the use of YOUR resources. Amen.

10/01/13 — **GOD**, I am not comfortable with "God language." I feel strange talking about YOU in such a public way. Yet the words will not stop coming. My heart hears YOUR voice and it begs to be shared. So comfortable or not, I will continue to defy my instincts to avoid "God talk" and go on sharing my personal experiences of being in YOUR care. YOU always figure into my actions and I cannot let YOU go. Please keep presenting YOURSELF to me in ways that startle and comfort and I will continue writing in the language of love that requires me to use "God talk." Amen.

10/02/13 — **Dear GOD**, YOU witnessed her tuck the card into my hand and YOU heard her say she was sorry for having smeared the ink. Her gift of the card was in thanks for giving her a medal I carry that reminds me to "Trust in the LORD always." It was a GOD moment. Thank YOU for a minute I will cherish forever. Amen.

10/02/13 — **GOD**, I thank YOU for teaching me to appreciate yoga. It stretches my body and it makes time to listen to YOU as I breathe. The steady rhythm of breathing and the pounding of my heart remind me of YOUR steadfast presence and grace in my life. I often feel like a fool when exercising. I am self-conscious but I know it is good for me. In much the same way, I am self-conscious about making a fool of myself for CHRIST. Nevertheless, if I can do the mountain pose and not fall over, surely I find the words to share the promise of YOUR son. I pray for courage, guidance, and I thank YOU for the insights of the day. Amen.

10/04/13 — **GOD**, we are blessed that You know and love us as no one else can. We don't have to present a résumé to work for You. Working for You allows us the freedom to love in our own style. You give us chances to grow and develop and YOU surprise us by showing accomplishments when we stop trying to be something we are not. We appreciate a leader who loves us wholly. May we work for YOU today and every day because that is the only work that allows us to become one with YOU. Amen.

10/04/13 — **GOD of the elements**, the rain and accompanying thunder and lightning are sounds that remind me of YOUR ability to grab our attention in flashy ways when we need to remember who is in charge. YOU don't expect or even demand that YOUR disciples light up the sky. YOUR only desire is that we make a CHRIST-like effort to profess YOUR love for all. So today, I will focus on moments where there is darkness and an opportunity to sow love. In CHRIST'S name, amen.

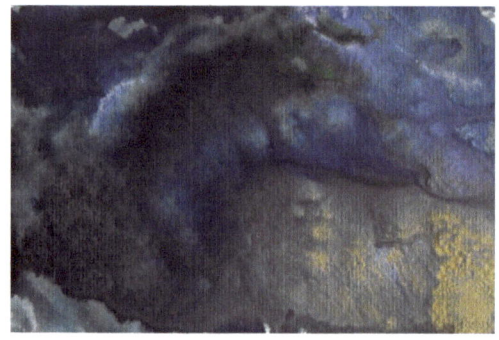

"Thunder"

10/05/13 — **Blessed Savior**, we often forget friends we made in earlier times in our lives. They change, we change, and sometimes we fail to recognize them when we see them at a class reunion. Today I was thinking about those people in our lives who are our "forever" friends. We can call them unexpectedly and pick right up where we left off.

YOU are the "forever" friend who never moved away—the friend who is with me every step of my life. Tonight I ask forgiveness for taking YOUR presence for granted. I live in grace because of YOU. I make mistakes and YOU love me still. I fail to listen when YOU offer YOUR guidance but because of YOU, I am redeemed. There is no better friend than YOU. Moreover, because of grace, I can say thank YOU and offer to be a better friend tomorrow. Amen.

"Where"

10/05/13 — **BLESSED SAVIOR**, my box of watercolors waited for me as I listened for directions. My mentor told me to take the brush and layer the paper with water and then to dig into a color and lay that color down on only a part of the paper. She kept saying "Dig for the color, really lay it down. Now choose another color and really dig, really lay it down. And finally, choose another color and really dig and lay it down." And then the directions got harder. She asked, "What color is missing? Why don't you add a little circle of that color and see what happens? Now take your brush and spread that color around as hard as you can."

And so I did, and so the morning continued. YOU were there, YOU saw the beginning creation, and YOU saw it through to the end. YOU heard her remind me to breathe. For the first time, I noticed that when I focus, I forget to breathe. I was practicing finding beauty and suddenly out of a chaotic mess, I found it. In addition, I was reminded that within chaos YOU are always there waiting to be discovered and claimed. I had to wait and wait and work and work and believe in order to uncover the beauty, but it was there—YOU were there. Amen.

10/08/13 — **Lord**, be with my friend who faces surgery today. Guide the hands and hearts of the surgeons. Your patient loves You and consistently walks in Your steps. All I can ask today is that those of us who love her surround her with prayer, and believe that You are with her no matter the outcome. Amen.

10/10/13 — **Dear God**, I love the beauty of autumn, not because of the purples and gold of leaves changing and the nip of cold in the early morning. I love this time of year because my life was blessed by You when my friend Bill, stopped in the middle of a walk and kissed me. It was a defining moment of love. That kiss was the glimpse of an adventure that has lasted more than 30 years. Sometimes, I thank You for silly things. Today, I thank You for Bill and his patience, his wisdom, and his love of You that gave him the courage to take a chance on love with me. Amen.

10/11/13 — **God of adventures**, today I await whatever You have in store for me. I may need to ask for help and forgiveness. No matter where I am, I know that at the end of the day I will offer thanks and praise for Your faithful presence. Amen.

10/12/13 — **God of all blessings**, thank You for the beauty of the day and small accomplishments. Thank You for letting us know that righteousness has no hierarchy and grace is available to all. In Your Son's name, amen.

10/12/13 — **Creative Maker**, we sometimes search and pray for new ways to express our creativity. We look at the actions and materials used by others and go home to re-examine what we have to work with. Suddenly, an accident happens in the studio and two things that shouldn't work get combined and work to create the beauty we were seeking. I believe it's a plan YOU have for leading us to look at old things in a new way. May we appreciate both the old and the new when they collaborate whether by intention or by accident. Amen.

10/14/13 — **Dear GOD**, thank YOU for the conversation found in art. Painting calls me into communion with YOU, and as a loving parent, YOU say to me "Tell me about this." As a loving friend, YOU urge me to post my work on the refrigerator. I am blessed with paint and brushes and a LORD who believes in creating. It's a fascinating experience to pray in color and to really know I am accepted for being "abstract." Amen.

10/15/13 — **LORD,** we know that YOU gifted us differently. May we consider differences when in conversations and meetings around the work of YOUR church? Some of us are gifted at strategy and less gifted in relationships. Others of us are learners through relationships. Give us the wisdom and the patience to stitch together a quilt of gifts that we will use to warm the sick, the lonely, the frightened, and the forgotten. Remind us that the most beautiful quilts consist of different patterns sewn together by many hands gathered around the quilt frame. In the work of church, YOU provide the frame, the patterns, and the hands. Show us how to layout and stitch diverse patterns into one cloth. Show us how to fit our gifts together to do YOUR will. Amen.

10/19/13 — **GOD**, tonight the prayer is simple. May we rest well and wake with passion and energy to do YOUR will. Open our eyes to those who need us and place us in spots where we can help. Amen.

10/20/13 — **GOD of early morning**, we face a day of surprises as we know the plans we make will change. Give us flexibility and patience when we end up at unknown destinations. May our hearts skip a beat when newness presents itself. May we walk hand in hand with YOU wherever we go. Amen.

10/21/13 — **GOD**, we see injustices creep into lives of the ordinary. Life becomes distorted and families are broken and driven to act in ways that inflict pain and anguish. Give us the voice of the widow, who unceasingly returned to the judge, until, exhausted by her tenacious faith, he removed the barriers to justice. Give us the faith of the widow and let us act in public ways, so that we might in some small way be justice in action. In YOUR SON'S name I pray, amen.

10/22/13 — **Gracious GOD**, thank YOU for the experiences that drive YOU into our lives. When we suffer, YOU are beside us cradling us as YOUR children. When we celebrate, YOU are the air that causes our balloons to float. When we come to YOU in prayer, YOU run to greet us as the father of a prodigal child. We are to imagine the world as YOU imagined it and we do this in joy and love and with the knowledge that if we stumble, YOU will pick us up and kiss our wounds and give us another chance. In CHRIST'S name, amen.

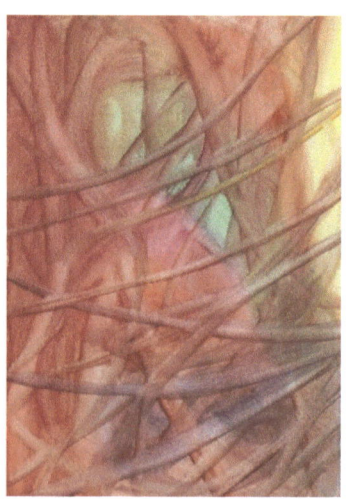

"Soaring"

10/23/13 — **GOD who loves parties**, we are YOUR family. We gather around a table spread with offerings made from recipes and memory. YOU find us at the campfire, and we see YOU as sparks fly upwards. We hear YOU in songs sung in voices both new and old. We feel YOUR warmth when we linger to see the last log turn to ashes. We know YOU as the loving parent who rejoices with us as we remember the ones whose chairs are empty now, but whose wisdom remains. We remember the story of the loaves and fishes, and are reminded of the power in potlucks. The feast at Cana reminds us of the joy found in celebrations. Give us courage to open our lives to those who feel they have nothing to offer the host. YOUR son, JESUS calls us to add extensions to the table and pull up more chairs. The presence of another is one more chance to be with YOU. Amen.

10/24/13 — **LORD GOD**, we give YOU thanks for times of change. The good things bring us joy. The ugly times give us wisdom to know that we will survive. Life is never ending transition. We may plant our feet, but the world moves anyhow. We are blessed to know that YOU share in our journeys and that, when this life ends, we come home to YOU! Amen.

10/25/13 — **Dear LORD**, I am constantly surprised by love and grace. Transitions in life are difficult and my daughter calls them challenges to be graceful. Yesterday, I provided my boss with opportunity to exercise grace and he was up to the task, repeatedly! Amen.

"Water"

10/27/13 — LAST OUTING WITH MOM

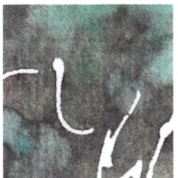**Dear God**, today was simple in its glory. She asked for a manicure/pedicure. The women in the shop treated her like a princess. As an act of worship, we took a ride to view brilliantly colored maple trees. You know she is nearly blind, but still sees color. She tells me she is satisfied with what remains. She reminds me to watch for deer, and, when we part at home, she tells me I may love her but she has loved me longer. I give You thanks for the day with Mom. Amen.

10/28/13 — **Holy Parent**, we thank You for beautiful colors and the contrast they present against the muted sky of fall. It reminds us to reflect and reach inside ourselves to find the various hues of what makes us up. We know we belonged in Your paint box once, and with Your paint brush You swept us off Your easel to bring life to Your vision. May we be brushed with kindness and humility, and remember that Your colors are never exhausted and we are blessed to be awash with Your love. In Christ's name, we pray, amen.

10/30/13 — **Dear God**, there was silence is the fog this morning. No sounds, only faint shadows and lights in the distance. The peace enveloped me and I breathed softly, so as not to wake any fellow commuters. I remembered that even in the grayness of a fog that does not allow us to see what lies ahead, we are sure in the knowledge that You wait with us to see the sun break through.

Thank You for mornings like this, when the world seems to slow to a stop and prayers from nature are reflected in the drizzle. Amen.

10/31/13 — **Dear GOD**, we pray for a safe journey tomorrow to see our daughter defend her dissertation. This commitment she made to research and writing is stunning, and we pray for a good outcome. Be with everyone tomorrow as they make life-changing decisions regarding careers. Amen.

11/01/13 — **Dear GOD**, we remember all the saints who bless our lives. Those still living and those who have come home to YOU. I thank you especially for Mary, Frank, John, Norma, Vincent, Richard, Bob, and my dad, Carl. I honor Irene and Jane, who are gifted at showing us what it means to live faithfully. This is my prayer. There are so many more, and may others add to the list. In CHRIST'S name, amen.

In Between

11/04/13 — **Giver of life**, we trust YOUR presence in all things. We rejoice in the love of family and the warmth generated by being in community when we can only guess at the future. We learn to leave expectations behind as we remember that CHRIST did not leave us comfortless. We pray for those who are afraid and only ask for a hand to hold. We thank YOU for those who have been and continue to be a constant blessing and fount of wisdom. May we parent our parent with the same selfless attention poured out on us. Bless us as we live in the present and hold us steadfastly as we experience each next step as it reveals itself to us. In CHRIST'S name we pray. Amen.

11/04/13 — **Dear GOD of hands**, I hold my mother's hand and remember the first day she walked me to school. She said I would love it and I did. I hold her hand and remember the books it held while she patiently read to us in the evening. I hold her hand and I remember her teaching us to pray with folded hands. I hold her hand and I remember it holding a fishing rod while I reeled in my first catfish. I hold her hands and I look upon the beautiful works of counted cross stitch on fabric so fine that YOU cannot tell it was done with thread and not paints. I hold her hands and I look around at the family who has gathered to wish her a good journey, and I see a new painting of family stitched together on a fabric of love that she herself wove for us. I am speechless at what hands can do; especially those hands that always held YOURS. We are holding her hands and telling her she's going to love the new destination, and we know she will. Thank YOU for giving her to us with hands so beautiful that nothing, not even letting them go, will separate us from YOU or her. In YOUR SON'S name we pray, amen.

NOTE: This prayer was read at her funeral by her granddaughter.

11/05/13 — **Holy ONE**, mom rests tonight—the first time since Friday. We have her pain under control and we thank YOU for that. This is a difficult time, and each of us is glad we are not only children. We pray for those who are, and who have to make tough decisions on their own. Our family is laced together in love by a wonderful mother who will tell YOU she messed up some of the time. We will tell YOU she has gotten it right most of the time. We have found our prayer to be short tonight. Please GOD, take away her pain. Amen.

11/05/13 — **God of journey**, we experienced joys and concerns today, and this time we remained present with the knowledge that You were with us. We abandoned fear of the future. And, oh how different the world looks when You wrap Your arms around us. Amen.

11/10/13 — **Dear God**, we know not what awaits us today. We are sure of only one thing—Your love for us. I pray for the continued love of family and friends and for the gifts of caregivers. I ask a special blessing for my mom. She is a fighter and hates to leave a party. I don't know what else to say except thank You. Amen.

11/11/13 — **Dear God**, You were with us when the time came to let her go. We watched as she came closer and closer to the last breath. She became our child, and we sang lullabies to calm her and help her sleep. We have sent her back to You. Let her be counted as one of Your saints. Amen.

11/12/13 — **Blessed Jesus**, the words are difficult to find tonight. The day was long and full of change. I tried to find You in my unfamiliar activities and I could not feel Your presence. I realized I was not breathing You. Please help me remember to anchor my life in You as I walk through grief. In Your presence and love I pray, amen.

11/13/13 — OBSERVATION

This morning I was dusting in order to remove fingerprints. Aside from having waited too long to dust, I thought about the fingerprints God leaves on every creation. The lesson is, we may dust, but we can never dust away the sacred. It makes doing the mundane tasks a chance for thanksgiving. Thank you, mom, for teaching me to keep a clean house.

11/13/13 — **Creator of humanity**, my mother's fingerprints are all over me and I know You created them. She was created in Your innermost being and she was knit together in her mother's womb. What a glorious fabric You wove her into. My heart is full of thanksgiving for her time with us. Amen.

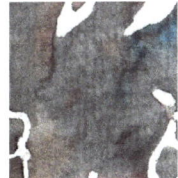

11/17/13 — **Dear God**, this is an in between time. Time, ordinarily broken up by routine, shifted. The days and nights are different and ritual reshaped. I picked up the phone to call her today and then I remembered that no one would answer.

This is an in between time—a time that is seemingly mystical and without direction. You equipped me for this time by surrounding me with family and friends bound together by love and concern.

This is an in between time—and I find a beauty in silence that I never appreciated as much as I do now. I know that You are present in this strange time. I see evidence in the rain and the sun, and the last leaves swirling in the air.

This very sacred time gives me the chance to say thank You for the moments of awe that could only have been produced by You. You are precious Lord. I give You my hand.

This is an in between time—amen.

11/19/13 — **Dear God**, we give You thanks for moments and events that free us up to greet the next adventure. Days of rest and time of reflection nurture our souls and renew our energies. There are those who suffer great anxiety today over issues of health that seem immense and unconquerable. Gently breathe Your presence into their hearts and hopes. Give them light to clear away the darkness that comes with fear of the unknown. We beg You in Your mercy to watch over them, love them, and restore them to health. We are confident in Your will and if we are required to surrender them to You, we do so with the knowledge that they will live with You forever. But in the meantime, let us be graceful in embracing the unknown. In Christ's name we pray, amen.

"Softness"

11/22/13 — **Dear God, Source of all life**, there must be no declaring that others are different. We waste time judging, only to find that we are not cast in the role of judge, but rather the role of Your child. May we be re-born without intolerances programmed in. God, we beseech You to give us another day of grace so that we may practice embracing our neighbors even when we are uncomfortable. In fact, may we be uncomfortable in loving. It is a sign of growing towards You. Amen.

11/22/13 — **Dear God of work**, I declared myself a free agent today. At the end of the year I will close the door on an engaging life of corporate work, and begin a new journey that doesn't include the ritual of daily donning business casual clothing. My heart dances in delight at the prospect of being present with those whose company no longer has to fit around my work schedule. I offer thanks to You and to a loving and supportive husband. Without the presence of You and Bill, my life would lack the excitement that keeps me fueled and creative.

If, in this prayer, I have forgotten to say thank YOU for bringing me the joy and challenge of incredible cohorts, let me say it now. My work families escorted me through a maze of projects and opportunities and provided continuous moments of learning and laughter. Blessings on them and safe keeping. I ask for nothing more in life than to continue in conversation with YOU and to revel in the deep relationships found in family and friends. Amen.

11/22/13 — **Dear GOD**, I hate the tears that come at times I least expect. I am frustratingly like a child who pitches a fit because mom has gone to the neighbors and she didn't take me with her. When I tell someone my mom died, they say I couldn't have been surprised. She was 96 after all. In my mind she is always young, and smart, and beautiful—and worn out.

"Last outing"

I am surprised that this passing, though long thought about, still startles me with its reality. Hands reach out, but they are not hers. I feel like a porcupine and not a person. I probably need a sign around my neck that says, "Gone fishing and when I find what I am fishing for, I'll get back to you." If my prickles hurt anyone GOD, please give me a pass. I am wallowing and she always gave me about a week of wallowing before she said "Let's re-do your living room and get a new perspective." And, now I know that I must re-do my living room so light returns and prickles fall away. I will put in a touch of yellow to remind me she was here. YOU feel my sorrow and YOU are with me and, GOD why can't I be satisfied? Amen.

11/30/13 — **Loving God**, when did I begin to pay attention to Your voice? Was it only this year or have I been listening all along? You soften my heart and strengthen my soul. You challenge me to graceful dances with those I fear. You extend Your hands to me in times of doubt and You leave signs of Your constant love in the faces of all I meet. I am not who I planned to be, but rather I am shifting towards who You crafted me to be. The freedom to let go and let You be my wisdom brings me peace and joy, hope and love. Thanksgiving never ends.

11/30/13 — **Dearest God**, You added a saint to Your choir today. Not only does she love music, she loves creating beauty out of nothing. She will stay up all night to make sure everything is perfect. She arrived in Your arms about 2 am. She had plans to oversee the transition of decorating the sanctuary, but I guess she decided we're in good hands—and besides, it was Betty's birthday and they hadn't seen each other for so long. I am betting Dick was there greeting her with roses and ready to talk through his plans for glamming up the next sunrise.

God, we will miss Irene. The beauty she brought to us was splendid. You take care of her and don't let her convince You that she has no experience in decorating. We did our best today to meet her standards in the hanging of the greens. We plan to do our best every day to honor Your wisdom in giving Irene to us and now we honor Your wish to have her back safely in Your heavenly realm. Irene, pure heart, gracious, loving, dear, dear friend, we know You remain with us and we will make sure every orb on a wreath is perfectly placed. Amen.

11/30/13 OBSERVATION

My dear friend Irene died on the day of the hanging of the greens. It had been her custom for more years than I know, to supervise and critique our work. I miss her so often the pain seems to be unceasing. Yet I know it was time to let her go.

12/13/13 — **GOD**, I experienced CHRIST'S presence in my life yesterday in the form of patience over anger. I thought about the wasted energy anger generates and so I took a deep breath and let CHRIST lead me to peace. Peace gave me the energy to let go of notions about another and gave me back the patience I so desperately needed in the moment. YOUR spirit is with me if I only listen. May today be filled with patience and peace, amen.

12/17/13 — **Dear GOD**, I refuse apologizing for sorrow. I give thanks for the many years of joy that made sorrow possible. I weep at the singing of *Silent Night* and l treasure the deeper experience it symbolizes. YOU were with us on the final phrase of this beautiful song when my mother experienced the joy of meeting YOU face to face—joy and sorrow, deeply woven into beautiful memories. I will not apologize for tears as they are now crystals decorating heaven's halls, amen.

12/17/13 — **Please GOD**, open our hearts as vessels to catch the tears of those who beg to know why there are empty chairs at so many tables. We pray for comfort and rest for those called to journey with broken hearts. We remain confident that YOU are the source of strength and that in the bleakness of loss YOU reveal YOURSELF through unexpected moments of joy. YOUR gifts are too marvelous for our imagination, so we wait. Amen.

12/22/13 OBSERVATION

On December 22, 1983, a very brave and loving man made a contract with me to love me for at least 50 years. We have loved, danced, sung, cooked, and cried our way through the first 30. Our daughters have been the beneficiaries of the family that Bill has quietly and consistently partnered in building. We have two extremely funny and wise grandchildren we love without reservation. William Evans had me with the valentine that said "Every time I think about you my crayons melt." Love is built on shared history and stories that are created out of everyday moments. The first 30 years have been the prelude for the next 20 (and more if we give up gluten.) I honor your love and treasure your faithfulness. Happy 30th anniversary, Bill.

12/24/13 — **Divine Creator**, angels hover in corners waiting. Shepherds watch flocks of restless sheep. Peasants and money changers apprehensively search for words to describe the tremors creeping into their hearts. The night darkens, stars rise and without fanfare a child escapes the womb of a thirteen-year old virgin. The labor is not over. We, left with the messy afterbirth of holy moments, hear the cries of YOUR child. Cries mixed with glorious singing of angels, the lowing of cattle, the murmurings of strangers who question the star blazing overhead. Blessed by the holy birth, we remember the voices of others whose cries in the night have not prompted such outpourings of love. In grace, give us YOUR hand to gather them in and swaddle them in YOUR love. Much work remains. We ask for help in the memory of YOUR SON'S birth, amen.

"Eyes"

12/25/13 OBSERVATION — ON THE FIRST CHRISTMAS WITHOUT MOM

In preparation for Christmas brunch, I placed an extra chair at the table. A chair filled with memories that are the most precious of gifts. We will not throw memories out with wrapping or tuck them away to pull out for company use. We will wrap ourselves in them and send our thanks to the giver who loved us enough to leave behind the chair and its contents.

12/28/13 — **Dear God**, I confess that I harbor anger when my life feels out of control, even when the choice to change has been my own. I confess that Your love for me takes me on journeys that seem impossible. And I confess that I will continue my travel into the joy that comes from Your light. Oh God, take away my anxiety about what I can't change and give me courage to let go of inner ugliness so that I may be an instrument of peace and joy for the rest of my days. Amen.

12/29/31 — **Omnipotent one**, the years of what felt like shoveling heavy, wet snow and dragging it in a briefcase draw to a close this week. The warmth of shared community is a fire I take with me as I walk out the door. Guardian angels, please make sure the revolving door works, and thrusts me into a more gentle world made from gifts long suppressed. Those gifts now drift before me as snowflakes. I thank the saints who guided me and made room in their lives to mentor a child who challenged the rules. I thank You, God, for teaching me to pray while walking around.

I admit to loving the moments of deep intimacy in sharing the ordinary and extraordinary moments of cohorts' lives; and how the brightest and best of them blessed, loved, and tolerated me. I was daily challenged to see how others see the world. May I ease into my waiting skin without a fight and be a passionate lover of all You make available. You are my rock and my salvation. I trust in the joy of discovery I will find when I hand over my security badge, the door spins for the last time and the next adventure begins. Amen

12/30/13 OBSERVATION

I am cleaning out my desk. Just have to come in for a few minutes tomorrow and I am done. Wow! 52 years of work completed. What a great run. Forgive me if I am smiling.

12/31/13 OBSERVATION

To my friends and family, I send a special greeting for the New Year and a thank you for the old one. This past year brought new meaning to words "journey and separation". Since August, you travelled without passport, to places in my heart and in my soul. I let you in on conversations with GOD that covered wide geography. If the territory was new to you, you prayed with me, and if you had already visited that place you moved on. I am blessed to have reconnected with old friends and accept invitations into the lives of new ones. I lost my aunt, uncle, mother and a best friend this year and YOU blessed me and my family. My tears continue to fall, but generally they fall in thanksgiving for the face of GOD that you each have revealed to me.

"Resolved"

I retired today to move to my real work—making the world a place where peace and justice are a reality and not a vision. I cannot do this alone, so I pray that you will continue to act in kindness and love and together we might may a difference. Happy New Year!

Passage of Mother

On December 31, 2012, the most precious woman in my life developed a cough. It wasn't her first, but at 95 it scared us. We (five girls and three boys) began to see the real possibility of the imminent loss of our mother. Her cough called for action and action meant a meeting designed to create a care plan acceptable to her and possible for us to implement. You see, she always took care of herself and everyone else. She lived comfortably in a retirement community and with pride reminded everyone that she lived in the "independent unit." The cough, diagnosed as pneumonia, required a delicate change in her daily routine. She accepted that short-term help would be pleasant to start and end her day. She readily accepted a dinner date each evening with one of her children.

"Resting"

The cough passed and with it her resistance to loving caregivers. She enjoyed conversation and companionship. Her mind, ever sharp, remained so and she shared stories of earlier years when prompted. Her children enfolded the caregivers into the family. Caregivers escorted her to family events and ensured that family members had moments to continue memory making. She refused help on Sundays because her routine included church going and spending the day with her youngest daughter and the "grand dogs." Additionally, Sunday afternoons meant brunch with her kids and a trip to the nail salon. Her only vanity was her beautiful hands. She loved the fuss the manicurists made over her. It tickled her to know they purchased a special pillow just for her pedicure chair, because she was so short her legs did not reach the foot soak. Her eyes were more than dim and her hearing was fading but those Sunday routines kept her in the world.

On the first of September we celebrated her promotion to 96. She partied in fine style at three separate events. She enjoyed the parties but expressed embarrassment at so much fuss. October rolled around with spectacular brilliance. Even with limited sight she could see color. And so, after a manicure on the last Sunday of October, we took a ride to the river for viewing of leaves. She "Oohed" and "Aahed" at the richness of the colors and the smells of fall. When asked how old she felt she replied "I guess about 40."

One thing skipped over was her diagnosis of mantle cell lymphoma eight years earlier—stage four. Given a very short life expectancy, she went about her business, and at age 90 refused to see the oncologist any more, as she felt great and thought it a waste of money.

On the morning of November 1, 2013, her caregiver found her asleep on the floor where she had fallen in the night. A trip to the emergency room indicated a broken color bone and shoulder. Nothing to get excited about she said that day. Her caregivers began round-the-clock care, supported at all times by family. Family members visiting from out of town headed for her headquarters to take on the privilege of personal care. As hours passed during the next week, her pain exceeded her comfort level, and clarity regarding the outcome of the fall brought extended family to her bedside. Hospice came at our beckoning and immediately she eased into the comfort of moving towards death.

On November 11, 2013, as a response to her children singing her favorite Christmas carol, she took her last breath on the lyric "Sleep in heavenly peace." Her entire adult life she expressed a wish to be a teacher. Her children, grandchildren and hundreds of others who were fortunate enough to know her, benefitted from her example of lifelong learning and loving. At the end, her last conversation included a question, "Are you all going to be okay?" Well, mom, we are. We honor your advice as follows:

1. When we go out, we wear underwear with no tears.

2. We watch for deer.

3. We love each other to the moon and back.

4. We remember that church won't hurt us.

Mom loved us as GOD loves his Son, and she shared her gifts in light—in life and now in death.

Caryn Evans

www.ingramcontent.com/pod-product-compliance
Lightning Source LLC
Chambersburg PA
CBHW041701160426
43191CB00002B/44